MEDICARE ENTITLEMENTS EXPOSED

HOW THE MEDICARE SAVINGS ACCOUNT WILL CHANGE HEALTHCARE DELIVERY IN AMERICA

GEORGE FOX

The opinions expressed in this manuscript are solely the opinions of the author and do not represent the opinions or thoughts of the publisher. The author has represented and warranted full ownership and/or legal right to publish all the materials in this book.

Medicare Entitlements Exposed
How the Medicare Savings Account will change healthcare delivery in America
All Rights Reserved.
Copyright © 2013 George Fox
v2.0

This book may not be reproduced, transmitted, or stored in whole or in part by any means, including graphic, electronic, or mechanical without the express written consent of the publisher except in the case of brief quotations embodied in critical articles and reviews.

Outskirts Press, Inc.
http://www.outskirtspress.com

ISBN: 978-1-4327-9946-5

Outskirts Press and the "OP" logo are trademarks belonging to Outskirts Press, Inc.

PRINTED IN THE UNITED STATES OF AMERICA

Contents

Introductions i
Chapter 1: How Did We Get Here? Mapping the History of Healthcare Legislation in the United States 1
Chapter 2: MSA in Focus: Highlighting Laws That Impacted the Medicare Savings Account or MSA.. 15
Chapter 3: Coordinated Care Plans: The Promise, The Problem 24
Chapter 4: Money, Money, Money: Get More and Keep More With the Medicare Savings Plan!.. 33
Chapter 5: Can I Really Do This? Opting Out of Coordinated Care is Easier Than You Might Imagine. (But There Are Some Rules.)... 43
Conclusions... 59
Bibliography 65
Suggested Resources 72
Where to get more information or enroll 74
Event Registration Form 76
About the Author 78

Introductions

THERE ARE SEEMINGLY endless uncertainties in life. One thing is almost certain for Medicare beneficiaries: you will face an unexpected health event.

Medicare is good coverage but it is not *complete* coverage. If you are a beneficiary of Medicare, you must decide whether you will retain the risks of unexpected health events or transfer them to an insurance carrier which will pay your claims as they occur.

The financial risk to the beneficiary inherent in the "Original Medicare" system demands that you buy secondary coverage to protect you from the risks of deductibles and co-insurance. That protection comes at a cost. The cost is the premium that you pay for the secondary coverage. Always keep in mind that a premium is, by definition, a known loss. You will pay your premium regardless of whether you use the coverage or not. This is similar to your homeowner's policy in that your pay a premium but your house has not burned down.

In the Medicare environment there are only really two ways in which you can eliminate the risks imposed by original Medicare coverage.

There are some people in the insurance industry who think that supplemental or secondary insurance is the only way to cover Medicare risks; in this format you can see any doctor who participates in the Medicare system. To follow their advice, you can take the traditional route of getting supplemental coverage. This will allow you to remain in Original Medicare and all of the deductibles and co-payments will be covered through the insurance carrier's policy when you choose the right policy. This format has existed from the very first days of the Medicare program in 1965.

On the other hand, there are those in the insurance industry who advocate for the use of Medicare Advantage plans which provide supplemental benefits above and beyond Original Medicare. Their position is that the additional benefits will out-weigh the restrictions of having to use a network plan or lacking non-emergency coverage when traveling out of your network.

This second option came through the 1997 Balanced Budget Act, which introduced Medicare + Choice. This legislation enabled beneficiaries to choose private coverage from commercial carriers instead of being covered by Medicare directly. As time passed the term "Medicare + Choice" became more commonly known as "Medicare Advantage" and that is the term that we use today.

The problem with considering the benefits and drawbacks of either of these options is that they offer a false set of choices. The fact is, (for reasons I will explain later in the book) both of these options are generally delivered through a managed or coordinated care model. It is simply a matter of "who" is coordinating your care. In both types of plan choices it will either be you or a benefit administrator. In the managed care plan model of coordinated care, your healthcare decisions are made for you. On the other hand, in a dynamic and innovative Consumer Directed Health Plan, you maintain control of your own healthcare decisions. The meaningful question is in fact not, which coordinated care plan to choose, but rather, whether to choose a coordinated care plan at all!

Many factors come into play in the development of healthcare options in the marketplace. Ultimately however, consumer demand drives the design of the Medicare system and how benefits are delivered. In my professional opinion, an effective model developed to meet consumer demand for improving access to healthcare without a managed care component is Consumer Directed Healthcare. This type of plan offers value and the greatest agency (that is, power!) for Medicare beneficiaries in the decision making process of healthcare choices. While most beneficiary-consumers rely on bureaucratically congested managed care plans, one type of Medicare Advantage plan, the Medicare Savings Account (MSA) provides a powerful mechanism to drive innovation in the coverage options available to all consumers. The MSA plan combines the best of Consumer Directed Healthcare with the added plus that it is funded by the Medicare system.

In this book I outline how this option emerged in legislative history, its comparative strengths over all other plans in the market, and the practical steps you can take to use it to your advantage.

CHAPTER 1

How Did We Get Here? Mapping the History of Healthcare Legislation in the United States

> This is an important hour for the Nation, for those of our citizens who have completed their tour of duty and have moved to the sidelines. These are the days that we are trying to celebrate for them. These people are our prideful responsibility and they are entitled, among other benefits, to the best medical protection available.
>
> President Lyndon B. Johnson's remarks with President Truman at the Signing in Independence of the Medicare Bill

July 30, 1965

These words spoken by the thirty-sixth president of the United States, Lyndon B. Johnson, in July of 1965 heralded the culmination of a mission that had started in 1910 with then presidential hopeful Theodore Roosevelt.

To fully understand that fifty-five year legislative journey and how we arrived at the system we have today, we need to understand the history of socialized medicine. Whether you think the idea of government-run healthcare is a good thing or not, the reality is that the government *is* running healthcare –directly or indirectly- through the regulation of insurance carriers and the providers of care. Given this fact, it is to your benefit to understand how certain laws came to be and how to apply them to your advantage.

The concept of a national healthcare system, in fact, dates back further than you might imagine. Universal healthcare traces its roots back to Europe and Germany under the rein of Otto Von Bismarck's Health Insurance Bill of 1883, the Accident Insurance Bill of 1884, and Old Age and Disability Bill of 1889 (Wikipedia).

That European concept of universal healthcare crossed the Atlantic and took hold in the United States and lingered in the consciousness of the political arena for many years. The first incarnation of a national healthcare system in the United States goes back to 1910 when presidential candidate Theodore Roosevelt proposed a system of national healthcare to cover all working Americans as part of his platform (National Public Radio, 2009).

The "Social Insurance Committee," which was formed by Congress in April of 1916, was tasked with the formation of a legislative proposal. That proposal was to create a Social Insurance program in the United States.

In testimony from Miles M. Dawson, who was a consulting actuary before the Committee on Labor in the House of Representatives in 1916, Dawson attributes many benefits to Germany as a whole due to the universal healthcare system. These benefits included prolonged life spans, higher national output of goods and services, a more effective military and various other benefits, as a result of the implementation of a National

Healthcare plan. (sounds familiar) Specially, he is quoted in his testimony as stating:

> I found, and I found later when I was there for a second time that the remarkable improvement in the efficiency of the people in connect with the industries of the counties, an increase in efficiency which, as you know, has attracted worldwide attention, which changed the reputation of German workman from that of a rather through but exceedingly slow and plodding type of workman, which was there reputation when I was a boy, to that of easily the most efficient workman in all of Europe, and made the Austrians in spite of the fact that they were so badly broken apart in regard to race conditions, only second to the Germans in that regard- that this increase in efficiency, while un-doughtily partly due to the introduction of special schools in Germany and Austria, meaning vocational education, and also partly due to the introduction of compulsory military service, and the creation thereby of a

special form of discipline was chiefly due to Social Insurance (Labor, 1916).

Over the years, the concept of a government-run health care system reemerged numerous times. However, it was under Harry Truman that the national healthcare system finally became what we call Medicare. This is the system that has been in use from 1965 until now, with several attempts at reform.

Dawson's statement highlights the fact that the pursuit of a national healthcare plan has always been driven by the desire to provide significant benefits to society as a whole. But these benefits come at a cost. Evaluating the cost of national healthcare against its benefits has always been- and will always be- the major legislative factor.

It was the projections concerning how the benefits for Medicare would be funded in later years that concerned legislators back then and this issue continues to plague us today. In fact, when Medicare was first conceived and passed into law, the serious mistake legislators made was not looking at the history of the German experience. In 1916 there was a documented 14-year increase of life span for the average German worker.

In 1965 the life span of an average American worker was 66.8 years of age. In fact, most workers died before any benefits were paid out for them. Today the average male will live to 83 years of age; a full 18 years longer than in 1965 when Medicare was signed into law. Is the extension of life spans because of the implementation of the Medicare system or just the result of medical care improvements? You can find conflicting studies on both sides of the debate. In the end, however, it is a moot point because the fact is that the average Medicare beneficiary will consume far more benefits than ever envisioned by the signers of the Medicare law (Administration).

The second conceptual legislative error was to build a program based on the assumption that there would be 4.5 workers for every Medicare beneficiary. Today, there are only 2.3 workers for every beneficiary on Medicare and that number is falling (Heritage Foundation, 2012).

As with many government programs, the burden for over-promises and underfunding come to roost on future generations. That is in fact, where we are today. Projected underfunding of the Medicare system is a significant issue for the system as it stands today. The legislative agenda in the past few decades has therefore centered on two questions: How to transfer the burden of paying for the ever increasing cost of healthcare from a government-run system to the consumers of that healthcare? How to empower those consumers to coordinate their own care while still keeping oversight so that the system will not spiral out of control?

Congress has attempted to pass laws that will provide financial solutions to these questions, often with little success. Successive congressional sessions have tried to fix what seems to be an insurmountable financial dilemma. Often, the approach has been to cut benefits and raise premiums on beneficiaries. This always results in a backlash from the public who will ultimately have to foot the cost.

When it comes to Medicare specifically, the legislative solution was on the books in 1997 in the form of Medicare Advantage plans. In creating the Medicare Advantage plan, Congress effectively created a solution to the problem of increasing costs and access to physicians at a reasonable price. Unfortunately, the popularity of managed or coordinated care took hold in the Medicare Advantage sector; providers of healthcare wanted to consolidate the control on the healthcare delivery system to their own benefit.

In creating these types of Medicare Advantage plans, which are commonly referred to as Health Maintenance Organizations (HMO), providers ensured that beneficiaries would stay within the systems that the plan created; with managed or coordinated care plans the beneficiary can only receive healthcare from providers in that HMO system. In the short-run, this appears to be to the benefit of providers because they do not have to compete in the market- place. They *are* the marketplace for consumers who choose to use this type of managed care plan. Additionally, the provider's revenue is assured regardless of where the beneficiary receives their care; it's a closed loop for the providers of care.

For the Medicare beneficiary however, the one overriding issue is mounting costs concurring with increasingly limited access to health care. Regardless of the size of the plan, the network will always strive to limit beneficiary access to providers within the system. To combat this negative feature, plans offer a Preferred Provider Network or PPO allowing beneficiaries to exit their network if they do need to see providers outside of the network system.

If the solution to the issue of access is to go get your healthcare where you want it, then why have a network at all? The answer is simple: Money! It generally costs the plan more to allow you to see any medical provider you want, as opposed to a network provider. This is because the network provider agreed to provide the same services at a reduced cost compared with the cost at which a non-network provider will provide those same services to the beneficiary. When we understand that it is always a cost issue, then we can understand why the Medicare Advantage plans want you to stay within the networks that are set up by the plans.

By establishing these networks, these plans have in fact, solved two issues with which all businesses must contend. First, networks provide a steady stream of consumers that are captive to the network. This network model effectively eliminates competition in the business model equation. The second benefit is that network participation provides a consistent revenue stream for the medical provider. Therefore networks work to the advantage of healthcare providers because it supplies the two things most needed: consumers of healthcare and consistent payment for services.

On the other hand, for the beneficiary in the Medicare system, the Managed Care model may not be so good. For the beneficiary, it limits the options they may choose from when seeking healthcare. This limitation may not seem so bad for the small things, but when you are facing significant healthcare issues, the last thing you want is to have some clerk telling you that you cannot go and see the physician that you want to see because they are not in the network.

Recently there was an attempt to implement what I would call a true National health care system under a bill called the "Expanded and Improved Medicare for All Act". This bill was introduced in the 113th Congress on February 13th, 2013 by Representative John Conyers Jr. and was co- sponsored by 42 other Representatives in Congress. If this legislation makes it through Congress and is signed into law, it will expand the current Medicare system to cover all citizens in a universal healthcare plan that provides the many benefits.

Yet the financial impact of such a law would be so widespread that it is impossible to foresee its true effects on the economy, providers of healthcare, and healthcare delivery systems as we know them today. Ambitious in its scope of coverage and far- reaching in the depth of those it would cover, those evaluating bill HR 676 would be well-served to review the lessons of history to understand the difficulties in achieving consensus among all those interested parties in such a massive undertaking.

Ultimately, those legislators who desire to avoid the repetition of past over-promising and underfunding will ultimately prevent the passing of the "Expanded and Improved Medicare for all Act".

It was the demand for cost reductions and better coverage that brought the preventive coverage provisions of the Medicare system being designed to offer all participants first dollar coverage for healthcare, making preventative care and early intervention the norm for all participants. The congressional sessions that enacted the Medicare Modernization Act, Affordable Care and Patient Protection Act did manage to deliver solutions for the vast majority of Americans to improve their coverage and hopefully reduce their insurance costs.

Well before the legislative debates we are witnessing today, it was in those Congressional sessions in 1997 that a Consumer Directed Healthcare option was made available through the Medicare Savings Accounts (MSA) and was first enacted as a demonstration or test program. At first, a little known and sparsely used program, this type of Medicare Advantage plan offered most Americans who qualified for Medicare a unique and affordable solution to their coverage needs when they entered the Medicare System.

It is essentially consumer demand that drives the design of the Medicare system and how benefits are to be delivered. As you go through this book, you will see how no one law provides a single solution, but it is the accumulation of consumer demand for improved coverage on successive congressional sessions that have formed what we now call Medicare benefits today. Nonetheless, it is the Consumer Directed Healthcare model that should be the preferred healthcare model for anyone who wants to control the how, when and where they receive their healthcare. An article from the American Academy of Orthopedic Surgeons clarifies what the term Consumer Direct Healthcare really implies:

> The phrase "consumer-directed health care" or "CDHC" is used synonymously in the current healthcare literature with terms such as "consumer-directed health plans" or "consumer-centric health care." Regardless of the terminology used, the concept is that patients ("consumers")

should have more control in the utilization of their healthcare dollars (Sharat Kusuma, Nunley, Covey, Genuario, & Mehta, 2008).

The Medicare Savings Account is a Consumer Directed Healthcare Model that is specifically designed for Medicare beneficiaries who want that control.

CHAPTER 2

MSA in Focus: Highlighting Laws That Impacted the Medicare Savings Account or MSA

The Affordable Care Act's emphasis on co-ordinating and integrating healthcare can conflict with government antitrust efforts."

"There is a tight balance between a coordinated care strategy and a monopoly" (Bird, 2013).

In this chapter I am going to highlight the laws most relevant to the Medicare Savings Account (MSA). Then I will discuss the impact these laws had on the Medicare system- whether intentional or not!

It all starts with the Balance Budget Act of 1997. Even though this law was, like many others, full of items unrelated to Medicare, it was here that the transformation of the Medicare system started. The Center on Budget and Policy Priorities wrote a very extensive overview of the law to which I will refer in this chapter. In dissecting that analysis, there is a significant emphasis on reducing the cost of the Medicaid system. Here are some excerpts:

> The legislation contains a dramatic expansion in state authority with respect to the use of managed care. It enables states to require most Medicaid beneficiaries to enroll in managed care organizations (MCOs) that only do business with the Medicaid program without obtaining a waiver from the Secretary of HHS…

> The legislation contains some new federal Medicaid expansions as well…

> The legislation establishes a new child health block grant, through which $20.3 billion in new federal funds will be made available to states over the next five years

for the purpose of reducing the number of uninsured low-income children.[5] This block grant has important implications for Medicaid. At a minimum, it gives states an incentive not to reduce their current Medicaid eligibility levels for children; states that adopt income or resource standards or methodologies more restrictive than those in effect on June 1, 1997 may not qualify for any federal child health block grant funds (Schneider, 1997).

Although not directly related to Medicare, this is a critical aspect of the legislation; notice specifically the provision for the expansion of managed care. This is similar in concept to what happened on the Medicare side of the legislation, except with Medicare, there could not be cuts or reduction *because the program is an entitlement.* What is an entitlement?

> The kind of government program that provides individuals with personal financial benefits (or sometimes special government-provided goods or services) to which an indefinite (but usually rather large) number of potential beneficiaries

have a legal **right** (enforceable in court, if necessary) whenever they meet eligibility conditions that are specified by the standing law that authorizes the program...

The existence of entitlement programs is mainly significant from a political economy standpoint because of the very difficult problems they create for Congress's efforts to control the exact size of the budget deficit or surplus through the annual appropriations process... the amount of money that will be required in the coming year to fund an entitlement program is often extremely difficult to predict in advance because the number of people with an entitlement may depend upon the overall condition of the economy at the time...

Perhaps more significantly, the amount of spending on entitlement programs is impossible for the Senate and House Appropriations committees to even attempt to adjust or to control because those committees do not have the jurisdiction to rewrite the laws that specify who gets how much and under what conditions. (Johnson).

So then, by definition, an entitlement program has unpredictable costs! What would make sense for the government to do to minimize the risks of an entitlement such as Medicare, which has ever-rising and unpredictable costs? The answer is very simple and so obvious when you understand the basic principle of insurance. When you purchase insurance, what you are really doing is *paying a known loss, the premium, to avoid an unknown loss.* In the case of Medicare, the Medicare system is entirely responsible for all part A and part B expenses incured by the beneficiaries, based on the coverage limits afforded by the Medicare system. Therefore, the government faces tremendous unknown and unpredictable risk in the course of fulfilling its obligation to deliver the Medicare benefits to which you are entitled. But, if the Medicare system could transfer that risk of your medical claims- just like you do with your homeowners insurance for example- then the cost would be predictable and known because there would be no claims exposure!

Well that was exactly the government's motivation in the creation of the Balance Budget Act of 1997. In the Act, the provision in Section 4001 (Establishment of Medicare+Choice Program) (CMS) created the mechanism to allow the Medicare system to transfer the risk and administration of the Medicare beneficiary's claims. This transfer of risk is achieved through the creation of the Medicare Advantage plans, which are administered by private insurance carriers. As long as the beneficiary voluntarily enrolls in the Medicare Advantage plan, then the entire Medicare system has only to pay a monthly amount, what is in effect, a monthly premium to the private carrier and the United States government is off the hook.

It is quite clear when evaluating Medicare legislation and the creation of the Medicare+Choice plans, that there is an attempt on the part of the legislative body to create the means and the laws that shift lower-income populations to Managed Care and to incentivize the transference of risk in the Medicare population to private insurers. Unfortunately, until now, the Medicare beneficiary was only given the choice of Managed Care. However, with the final implementation and actual introduction in the later part of 2011, it is only now with the Medicare Advantage Medicare

Savings Account, the consumer directed healthcare plan is a reality.

The next law we will be looking at that had a significant impact on the Medicare system is the "Medicare Prescription Drug, Improvement, and Modernization Act of 2003" (US Congress, 2003) In this law, which is massive in its scope and quite frankly, mind-bending to read, I want to focus on just a few provisions.

The most important part of this section is that the Medicare Savings Program, which until then was a "Demonstration Program" for only 390,000 individuals, became permanent in the law. As previously discussed, it is really not until this radical shift that the actual MSA MA plan could exist. Until then, MSA MA plans were in practice, really not offered because no plans existed which were approved by Medicare that met the definition of a High Deductible Health plan *and* there really was no carriers that would commit to a plan that was on a demonstration basis.

The next section that is really the best know part of the act was Section 101. In this section we see for the first time the enactment of the Part D,

Medicare Prescription Drug Benefit. This part of the Medicare program is significant, because in essence, *you are seeing the privatization of a governmentally controlled program*. In other words, the Part D drug benefit that is part of the law that controls your Medicare Benefits is entirely run by private insurance carriers who voluntarily submit to being controlled by the Terms and Conditions set by the United States Government and the Medicare System. The Government, in exchange for providing, what is in effect, a privatized monopoly on the Medicare population benefits, relieves itself of the financial burden of administering a massive and (as we now know about entitlements) unpredictable cost. The Medicare system achieves this by simply contracting with private commercial insurance carriers to deliver the part D benefits.

What is important here is, unlike the implementation of the years prior, of the Medicare+Choice plans where you could stay in the "Original Medicare program" or voluntarily move to a private plan through choosing a MA plan, now, there is no government program. It is only a commercially run program under the control of the government. The second part of this is that all Part

D drug plans are essentially Consumer Directed Health Plans because it is the consumer who has complete choice over plan choice, plan pricing and weather to use the plan or not. The entire Part D benefit programs use is under the control of the beneficiary. Moreover, as we have seen in the later years of the program, the benefits are being amended to close the gap or "Donut Hole" in the plans because of the demand of Medicare beneficiaries. Although slow in coming, the gap is being closed and will be eliminated by 2020. *This is a direct result of consumer demand for innovation and improvement in the program. Make no mistake- consumers have power to shape their choices!*

How incredible that this option was "on the books" long before the present legislation came to pass! But before we get into the real solution to providing high quality healthcare, let's look at the healthcare delivery model that is most favored by the insurance industry and providers of healthcare alike.

CHAPTER 3

Coordinated Care Plans: The Promise, The Problem

> Our results suggest that care coordination, as practiced by the programs participating in the demonstration from 2002 to 2006, holds little promise of reducing total Medicare expenditures for beneficiaries with chronic illnesses (Randall Brown, 2009).

So why then did the Medicare Savings Account plan go unused by most insurance carriers in favor of the Managed Care Model of Medicare Advantage plan? The answer is simple: control and money.

There are many ways to deliver affordable and accessible healthcare to all Americans who want and need it. The "solution" that was seized on by the healthcare and the insurance industry was the Coordinated Care Model. Why that is, is really obvious when you accept the fact that healthcare is a business like any other type of business.

The name, *Coordinated Care*, implies a level of care that is organized and efficient, getting you where you need to be, seeing who you need to see, and getting all of the services you need under the umbrella of a healthcare manager who is looking out for you. It *sounds* good in theory. The problem, however, is that your healthcare needs do not play out on a spreadsheet or stump speech. In the real world you need a plan that delivers healthcare in a manner that is responsive to your dynamic and individualized needs.

Unfortunately in the case of Coordinated Care, you and your needs take a backseat to the needs of payers (insurance companies) and providers (healthcare professionals). While consumer demand drives Medicare reform, other parties' special interests can also hijack the process of reform. The coordinated care or managed healthcare model was ultimately developed to protect the financial interests of the insurance carrier and healthcare provider- not your healthcare needs.

The administration of your healthcare is broadly provided by an insurance carrier; however, most everyone does not want the insurance carrier in the decision making-process because the carrier imposes all kinds of rules and restrictions. It's not that the insurance carrier is trying to hurt anyone; as with any other business, they are simply seeking their own interests by reducing costs and managing utilization of services to maximize the benefits provided by the healthcare insurance policy.

Another factor in this type of plan configuration is the fact that the Independent Practice Associations (IPA) want to make money as well. What is an IPA? The best explanation of the IPA model is this: doctors form IPAs to negotiate better deals with insurance companies. IPAs and insurance carriers are at odds because while insurance carriers want to reduce costs, IPAs want effectively to increase insurance carrier costs by raising their fees. Therefore carriers and providers end up competing against one another for a greater share of the pie rather than focusing on how to most efficiently deliver the highest quality healthcare.

Now, money is not a bad thing! In fact carriers, doctors, and hospitals alike, need to be profitable and solvent so that they will be there when you need them. In fact, I would go so far as to say you should want your local physician or regional hospital to be wildly successful in a financial sense! The reason I say that is because when a business, which healthcare is, makes money, the provider of that care will reinvest in their business and innovate to improve care and reduce costs to their customers. This is the way all successful businesses operate to grow and attract more customers. Coordinated Care really has not provided any significant improvements in healthcare delivery under the Medicare system. This model of healthcare is actually counterproductive to encouraging innovation and improved quality of care. In fact, I would argue that it has created substantial barriers to improving care by adding unnecessary additional layers of bureaucracy which slow or prohibit access to care.

And, while some competition drives innovation, the wrong kind of competition can gum up the system. For example when IPAs and insurance carriers compete, this is a bad mix for the "end user," which is the beneficiary- you!- because the carrier is trying to restrict usages to lower costs, the providers are trying to increase costs to make more money.

When others' financial interests are prioritized out of balance with your dynamic and individualized needs, there is a problem. After all, the only purpose for having a healthcare system to begin with is to efficiently deliver healthcare- to you!

The most common form of the Coordinated Care plan is called a Health Maintenance Organization or HMO. This is a traditional network-restricted Coordinated Care Plan. A second type of plan Coordinated Care Plan which has come into favor is the Preferred Provider Organization or PPO. This type of plan has almost all of the same features as the HMO except it allows members to go outside of the "network" when they desire to do so- but this choice will result in higher costs to the consumer. Also, PPO's do not require referrals from primary care doctors but simply require you to stay within the network when seeking specialized care. So when you want to see, for example, that ear nose and throat doctor, you don't need to be referred by your primary doctor. You can in effect, coordinate your own care. You can also ignore the network all together but you will pay more out of pocket costs to use providers who have not agreed to belong to the network and provide services at a reduced cost. Therefore, it makes no sense to choose a PPO in order to be free to go "out of network," because joining a network plan so that you can go out of the network is counterproductive to the whole concept of having a networked plan under the Coordinated Care model! Think about it! If you join a PPO because you can go out of network, then why have the network plan at all. If you joined a PPO because you don't want to get referrals from a primary care doctor, you are in effect, coordinating you own care. You are your own healthcare manager.

  If you consider all of the issues related to the Coordinated Care model which include restriction on care, doctors who are trying to make more money by forming IPA's, and your desire to make healthcare decisions without the restrictions of the HMO or PPO models of healthcare, ultimately you can only come to the conclusion that Consumer Directed Healthcare is the only real solution. Consumer Directed Healthcare is the model that delivers all of the good features that you want with none of the drawbacks that you don't like. So what is a Consumer Directed Healthcare Plan? A Consumer Directed Healthcare Plan provides choice with none of the restrictions that are typical of a Managed Care Plans.

There is only one type of healthcare plan that was brought into existence by law that provides this kind of flexibility and coverage options that people need and want in a healthcare plan. That plan is a Medicare Savings Account which is the plan that was first introduced in 1997 as part of the Balance Budget act of 1997 and is public law 105-33.

The MSA Medicare Advantage plan is a superior choice in Medicare coverage for a variety of reasons, the most striking aspect of the MSA MA plan is that *it is not managed or coordinated healthcare*. It is Consumer Directed Health Care; it puts you in control!

The Medicare Savings Account Medicare Advantage plan restores the choice in healthcare decisions because it is a Consumer Directed Healthcare plan. This type of plan combines a High Deductible Health Care plan or HDHP plan with a medical expense savings account or MSA that is used to pay all Part A and Part B medical expenses from the first dollar.

The Medicare Advantage MSA plan empowers the Medicare beneficiary with total control over the who, where, what and when of their healthcare. Moreover, when you participate in a Medicare Advantage MSA plan the carriers and medical providers must compete for your business. They will do that by providing better care, more affordable care and be required to innovate or be driven out of the healthcare business.

When you want all of the benefits provided by unrestricted healthcare access and you want to be in control of your healthcare decisions, it is the Medicare Savings Account or MSA that offers the best solution in today's evolving healthcare arena. It has been in existence since 1997 and yet is virtually ignored by the healthcare industry!

While in the short-term, this poses additional challenges to carriers and providers, in the long-run, forcing them to provide better solutions to your healthcare needs which in turn makes them more productive businesses. Therefore, while Coordinated Care plans are to no one's benefit in the long-run, the Medicare Savings Account plan benefits the entire system. However, what you are (or should be!) most concerned with is how this plan is to your advantage. This is what I will discuss in the next chapter.

CHAPTER 4

Money, Money, Money: Get More and Keep More With the Medicare Savings Plan!

"We are giving Medicare beneficiaries the option of health savings account-type plans, as an additional choice among other health plan options in Medicare," (CMS Office of Public Affairs, 2006)

Hopefully, after reading all of the information presented in the previous chapters you have come to the same conclusions that I did after almost three decades in the insurance industry. The choices that you make to eliminate the risks inherent to being covered by Medicare are a simple economic calculation. For the most part, the choices you have been offered were developed to the economic benefit of the providers of the medical care or a third party or an insurance carriers. These groups are not trying to do bad things to you. They are simply working within the confines of a program or system to maximize the benefits that favor them. They, like you, seek out the advantages of one type of insurance program or law and use it to their fullest advantage. These groups are not obligated in any way to inform you that there is a better choice than the one they want you to use. My job *is* to show you every possible type of option available in order to eliminate the risks associated with being covered by Medicare.

I am confident that by now, you have reached the same conclusions that I did so very long ago. T*he Medicare Savings Account is by far the superior plan design for all of the right reasons.*

As discussed in previous chapters of this book, Coordinated Care is designed to serve the needs of the insurance carriers that provide this type of plan and sometimes the physician who participates in this type of plan. *It is not designed to serve the needs of the patient for one major reason: the patient has given up control or direction over their healthcare decisions to a plan administrator or provider network.*

This is the essence of consumer directed health care and why the MSA Medicare Advantage plan is the choice for individuals who are concerned with rising healthcare costs and want to be actively engaged in the process of reforming the healthcare system. When you make the right choice in a Medicare Advantage plan, your choice will help to shape even better future choices that will be available.

But let's be honest. Shaping the future is fine but what you really care about is the bottom line.

The fact is, you ought to choose the Medicare Savings Plan based on the superior advantage it offers in costs alone. Yes, the MSA is a Consumer Directed Health Plan that let you see any doctor that you want anywhere in the county. This fact makes it far superior to any form of Coordinated Care Plan because there are no restrictions on who can provide you healthcare. Yes, your physician will be paid at the standard rate that Medicare allows for services so he will be financially viable in the future and be practicing medicine when you need his services.

Furthermore, the Medicare Advantage plans available from most insurance carriers often enter the marketplace by having what is referred to a Zero Plan Premium. Unlike the HMO or PPO type of plans that initially start out as zero plan premium plans, the MSA carrier charges a zero plan premium because like all Medicare Advantage Plans in the market place, the Center for Medicare and Medicaid or CMS *pays the premium for the account holder.* The MSA carrier can, however, use the deductible to *keep* the premium at *zero dollars.*

In other words, when you choose the MSA Medicare Advantage plan you are essentially given a "Zero Plan Premium" for your healthcare plan because there is no premium to pay in the first place! In addition, you get all the same benefits and protections of Original Medicare! The only difference is that these benefits and protections will be delivered through a Medicare contracted provider, which is a Medicare Advantage plan.

Yes, with this type of Consumer Directed Health Care, when you manage the funds in your MSA account in a responsible manner and shepherd your resources to yield a surplus at the end of the year, you get to keep those dollars and use them in subsequent years.

Moreover, there are very few items in the tax code that can boast that the earning on your deposited funds have no taxable income consequences to the account holder when used according to the rules set in the law. There are but a few items that actually allow you to receive money into an account that is in your name without requiring you to pay income tax on that deposit. "It sounds too good to be true!" is the phrase that I hear most often when I tell Medicare beneficiaries that they can have an MSA and that is how it works. But it's true!

The Medicare Savings Account that is set up when you enroll in a Medicare Savings Account Medicare Advantage plan is one of the most unique values in healthcare you will ever find in today's maze of Medicare Advantage plans. In the next chapter I will review the tax rules that apply to the MSA MA plan and the unique features of the Internal Revenue Code. I will also outline the simple steps that are required to keep this money tax free.

At this juncture, I want to clarify what taxation is really all about in the modern world. If it was just about paying off the debt of the nation, we could just raise the tax rate to pay off all the debt in one year and be done with all this talk of national debt, right? But that is not what the tax system is all about in the end. Taxes are about incentivizing or disincentivizing behaviors of rational adults. Yet, whatever our philosophical or political beliefs about taxation, when most of us see a taxation rule or a favorable tax item that can reduce our income taxes or even avoid then out right, we consider that option very favorably. In the case of a Medicare Savings Account, the legislation that enacted the MSA and IRS enforcement of that law are so powerful that I doubt if there is any other tax provision that gives so much and takes virtually nothing out of your pocket.

But put all of those benefits of the MSA aside for a moment and just take a look at the total cost of all Medicare plans from a catastrophic perspective.

After all, why does a person have insurance coverage? To limit the personal financial exposure to medical claims. In the following chart, I have taken all of the costs associated with medical claims under the Medicare system. I compared the most common plans in the market with what is called the total out of pocket exposure of all types of plans. That includes Medicare Supplements and Medicare Advantage plans alike. Keep in mind that the payment of a premium is an out-of-pocket cost and is therefore included in this chart.

The chart includes deductibles, co-payments, out of pocket maximums and premiums in the combined total of some of the most common plans on the market for 2013. *Take any single component that relates to the insurance coverage and the MSA will always be the plan that will have a clear out of pocket cost advantage over any other plan type.*

At this point you might be wondering why you have never heard of such a great program. How could you have missed this option? Here is what the instruction manual provided by the IRS says about Medicare Savings Accounts:

> A Medicare+Choice MSA is an Archer MSA designated by Medicare to be used solely to pay the qualified medical expenses of the account holder who is eligible for Medicare. No Medicare+Choice MSAs have been established as of the revision date of this publication. Archer MSAs and Medicare+Choice MSAs are "pilot projects" scheduled to end December 31, 2002." "At the time this publication went to print, no HDHP had been <u>approved by Medicare</u>.

Therefore, no Medicare+Choice MSAs have been established to date (IRS, 2001).

So as you can see, the laws existed, but in 2001 there were no plans that could be used in relation to the existing laws! I point this out specifically because I want to illustrate with the inefficiency of massive federal agencies. Furthermore, while the Medicare Savings Account was made permanent in the law in 2003, it was not until 2011 that the second piece of the equation was put in place in New York State, *with the introduction of a High Deductible Medicare Advantage plan*. The introduction of that plan has paved the way for a revolution in the way healthcare is delivered to Medicare beneficiaries!

Yet, even today, the IRS provides little information regarding the tax code incentives in participating in this program. For example, in one tiny paragraph in IRS resources published in 2012 it states:

> A Medicare Advantage MSA is a tax-exempt trust or custodial savings account that you set up with a financial institution (such as a bank or an insurance

company) in which the Medicare program can deposit money for qualified medical expenses. The money in your account is not taxed if it is used for qualified medical expenses, and it may earn interest or dividends (IRS, 2012).

What, that's it? That's right! That's all the "blink and miss it" information provided on this provision in the tax code that puts FREE money in your pocket from the government to pay for your healthcare *and* earn interest and dividends on that money tax free and then spend the principle and earnings on your healthcare and pay no tax on those monies.

The fact is that there is so little information in the tax code concerning the filing requirements for MSA the Internal Revenue Service simply refers to the rules for "Health Savings Accounts and other Tax Favored Health Plans". Tax favored, well that is an understatement!

CHAPTER 5

Can I Really Do This? Opting Out of Coordinated Care is Easier Than You Might Imagine. (But There Are Some Rules.)

> "One independent group actually called this myth the lie of the year. The affordable Care Act put people, not health insurance companies or government, in charge of healthcare." (Whitehouse)

The most dominant model of healthcare delivery in the Medicare arena is the Coordinated Care Model. The concept of coordinated care is actually a noble and good concept. But the concept of offering "coordinated care" as a service obscures the fact that you are already coordinating your care yourself! You are already the best advocate for your health! Each time you seek out medical care from providers or service facilities without the intervention of a case manager, you are coordinating your own care.

But what about the nitty-gritty?

So as to be a clear as possible, I will outline the structure of the Medicare Savings Account and the two parts that make up the entire plan.

Part one is a special type of high deductible medical plan that covers all of your part A and part B costs at one hundred percent after you meet the annual deductible.

Part two is a savings account that is funded each year on January 1st by the MSA plan with a fixed amount of money. The deposited funds are immediately available for use by the Medicare beneficiary to cover any and all Part A and Part B medical costs within the calendar year.

Unlike any other type of Medicare Advantage plan that uses the Managed Care model, as previously discussed, with the MSA you are in control of your healthcare expenditures and the providers of your medical care during the calendar year.

The Medicare Savings Account plan is simple to use. There are, however, some basic steps that you need to know in order to successfully operate this type of medical plan.

To truly illustrate the MSA plan, I will discuss the specifics of a MSA plan for any state that the MSA MA plan exists. However, you should always consult with your insurance and tax advisors to ensure that you know all of the rules in your state.

First, you must establish a High Deductible Health plan with a contracted provider of a Medicare Savings Account Medicare Advantage plan.

The contracted provider will set up your Medicare Savings Account for you and fund it with your annual deposit.

The deposited funds and the interest earned in your MSA account are not subject to taxes as long as you use the money for healthcare costs as defined by the Internal Revenue Service. You can also use the money in your account for items that are not covered by Medicare Part A or B., like hearing aids, dental procedures and vision services. However, these types of expenditures will not be counted toward the reduction of your annual MSA deductible.

If you spend all of your funds in the Medicare Savings Account within the calendar year, you will pay for your own expenses until you reach the deductible within the calendar year. During the time you are paying directly for your part A and B, providers of Medical services, which includes doctors, laboratory and hospitals, but these providers cannot charge more than the Medicare approved amount.

After your deductible is met within the calendar year, the High Deductible Health Plan will pay one hundred percent of all Part A and Part B expenses for the remainder of the calendar year.

This means that you are never at risk for more than the difference between the MSA deposited money and the calendar year deductible as long as you only pay for Part A and B expenses from the MSA account.

This is a powerful way for you to control your costs and still keep control of the medical care you are receiving.

When using an MSA Medicare advantage plan, you must be aware of what is considered a "qualified" medial expense. As stated in the Medicare handbook:

> A Medicare Advantage MSA is an Archer MSA designated by Medicare to be used solely to pay the qualified medical expenses of the account holder. To be eligible for a [Medicare] Advantage MSA, you must be enrolled in Medicare and have a high deductible health plan (HDHP) that meets the Medicare guidelines. A Medicare Advantage MSA is a tax-exempt trust or

custodial savings account that you set up with a financial institution (such as a bank or an insurance company) in which the Medicare program can deposit money for qualified medical expenses. The money in your account is not taxed if it is used for qualified medical expenses, and it may earn interest or dividends (IRS, 2013).

If you spend the MSA deposited funds for any purpose that is considered "non-qualified" then you will be subject to a 50% tax penalty on those spent funds in the year in which you take the withdrawal. An examination of IRS publication 502 explains "qualified" to mean:

> Qualified medical expenses are those expenses that would generally qualify for the medical and dental expenses deduction. These are explained in Publication 502, Medical and Dental Expenses. Also, non-prescription medicines (other than insulin) are not considered qualified medical expenses for HSA purposes. A medicine or drug will be a qualified medical expense for HSA purposes only if the medicine or drug requires a prescription, Is available

without a prescription (an over-the-counter medicine or drug) and you get a prescription for it, or is insulin. You cannot treat insurance premiums as qualified medical expenses unless the premiums are for Long-term care insurance (IRS, 2013).

In addition to knowing what expenses are qualified, you should also be aware that each year you will receive a 1099-SA form from the bank acting as the custodian for your Medicare Savings Account. Because the IRS is responsible for tracking the tax-exempt status of your MSA deposits and expenditures, you must file an individual 1040 each year with the appropriate form 8853. There is no exception to this filing requirement as stated in the instructions.

You must file Form 8853 if any of the following applies.

You (or your employer) made contributions for 2012 to your Archer MSA. You are filing a joint return and your spouse (or his or her employer) made contributions for 2012 to your spouse's Archer MSA.

You (or your spouse, if filing jointly) acquired an interest in an Archer MSA or a Medicare Advantage MSA because of the death of the account holder. See Death of Account Holder, later.

You (or your spouse, if filing jointly) were a policyholder who received payments under an LTC insurance contract or received any accelerated CAUTION! death benefits from a life insurance policy on a per diem or other periodic basis in 2012…

You (or your spouse, if filing jointly) received Archer MSA or Medicare Advantage MSA distributions in 2012 (IRS, Instructions for Form 8853, 2012).

If you (or your spouse, if filing jointly) received Archer MSA or Medicare Advantage MSA distributions in 2012, you must file Form 8853 with a Form 1040 even if you have no taxable income or any other reason for filing Form 1040 (Medicare MSA booklet).

Form **8853**	**Archer MSAs and Long-Term Care Insurance Contracts**	OMB No. 1545-0074
Department of the Treasury Internal Revenue Service (99)	▶ Information about Form 8853 and its separate instructions is available at *www.irs.gov/form8853*. ▶ Attach to Form 1040 or Form 1040NR.	**2012** Attachment Sequence No. **39**

Name(s) shown on return	Social security number of MSA account holder. If both spouses have MSAs, see instructions ▶	

Section A. Archer MSAs. If you have only a Medicare Advantage MSA, skip Section A and complete Section B.

Part I   **Archer MSA Contributions and Deductions.** See instructions before completing this part. If you are filing jointly and both you and your spouse have high deductible health plans with self-only coverage, complete a separate Part I for each spouse.

1	Total employer contributions to your Archer MSA(s) for 2012	1	
2	Archer MSA contributions you made for 2012, including those made from January 1, 2013, through April 15, 2013, that were for 2012. Do not include rollovers (see instructions)	2	
3	Limitation from the Line 3 Limitation Chart and Worksheet in the instructions	3	
4	Compensation (see instructions) from the employer maintaining the high deductible health plan. (If self-employed, enter your earned income from the trade or business under which the high deductible health plan was established.)	4	
5	Archer MSA deduction. Enter the **smallest** of line 2, 3, or 4 here. Also include this amount on Form 1040, line 36, or Form 1040NR, line 35. On the dotted line next to Form 1040, line 36, or Form 1040NR, line 35, enter "MSA" and the amount	5	
	Caution: *If line 2 is more than line 5, you may have to pay an additional tax (see instructions).*		

Part II   **Archer MSA Distributions**

6a	Total distributions you and your spouse received in 2012 from all Archer MSAs (see instructions)	6a	
b	Distributions included on line 6a that you rolled over to another Archer MSA or a health savings account. Also include any excess contributions (and the earnings on those excess contributions) included on line 6a that were withdrawn by the due date of your return (see instructions)	6b	
c	Subtract line 6b from line 6a	6c	
7	Unreimbursed qualified medical expenses (see instructions)	7	
8	**Taxable Archer MSA distributions.** Subtract line 7 from line 6c. If zero or less, enter -0-. Also include this amount in the total on Form 1040, line 21, or Form 1040NR, line 21. On the dotted line next to line 21, enter "MSA" and the amount	8	
9a	If any of the distributions included on line 8 meet any of the **Exceptions to the Additional 20% Tax** (see instructions), check here ▶ ☐		
b	**Additional 20% tax** (see instructions). Enter 20% (.20) of the distributions included on line 8 that are subject to the additional 20% tax. Also include this amount in the total on Form 1040, line 60, or Form 1040NR, line 59. On the dotted line next to Form 1040, line 60, or Form 1040NR, line 59, enter "MSA" and the amount	9b	

Section B. Medicare Advantage MSA Distributions. If you are filing jointly and both you and your spouse received distributions in 2012 from a Medicare Advantage MSA, complete a separate Section B for each spouse (see instructions).

10	Total distributions you received in 2012 from all Medicare Advantage MSAs (see instructions)	10	
11	Unreimbursed qualified medical expenses (see instructions)	11	
12	**Taxable Medicare Advantage MSA distributions.** Subtract line 11 from line 10. If zero or less, enter -0-. Also include this amount in the total on Form 1040, line 21, or Form 1040NR, line 21. On the dotted line next to line 21, enter "Med MSA" and the amount	12	
13a	If any of the distributions included on line 12 meet any of the **Exceptions to the Additional 50% Tax** (see instructions), check here ▶ ☐		
b	**Additional 50% tax** (see instructions). Enter 50% (.50) of the distributions included on line 12 that are subject to the additional 50% tax. Also include this amount in the total on Form 1040, line 60, or Form 1040NR, line 59. On the dotted line next to Form 1040, line 60, or Form 1040NR, line 59, enter "Med MSA" and the amount	13b	

For Paperwork Reduction Act Notice, see your tax return instructions.   Cat. No. 24091H   Form **8853** (2012)

Form 8853 (2012) Attachment Sequence No. **39** Page **2**

Name of policyholder (as shown on Form 1040) | Social security number of policyholder ▶

Section C. Long-Term Care (LTC) Insurance Contracts. See **Filing Requirements for Section C** in the instructions before completing this section.

If more than one Section C is attached, check here . . . . ▶ ☐

14a Name of insured ▶ _____ **b** Social security number of insured ▶ _____

15 In 2012, did anyone other than you receive payments on a per diem or other periodic basis under a qualified LTC insurance contract covering the insured or receive accelerated death benefits under a life insurance policy covering the insured? . . . . ☐ Yes ☐ No

16 Was the insured a terminally ill individual? . . . . ☐ Yes ☐ No
Note: *If "Yes" and the **only** payments you received in 2012 were accelerated death benefits that were paid to you because the insured was terminally ill, skip lines 17 through 25 and enter -0- on line 26.*

17 Gross LTC payments received on a per diem or other periodic basis. Enter the total of the amounts from box 1 of all Forms 1099-LTC you received with respect to the insured on which the "Per diem" box in box 3 is checked . . . . | **17** |

Caution: *Do not use lines 18 through 26 to figure the taxable amount of benefits paid under an LTC insurance contract that is not a **qualified** LTC insurance contract. Instead, if the benefits are not excludable from your income (for example, if the benefits are not paid for personal injuries or sickness through accident or health insurance), report the amount not excludable as income on Form 1040, line 21.*

18 Enter the part of the amount on line 17 that is from **qualified** LTC insurance contracts . . . . | **18** |
19 Accelerated death benefits received on a per diem or other periodic basis. Do not include any amounts you received because the insured was terminally ill (see instructions) . . . . | **19** |
20 Add lines 18 and 19 . . . . | **20** |
Note: *If you checked "Yes" on line 15 above, see **Multiple Payees** in the instructions before completing lines 21 through 25.*

21 Multiply $310 by the number of days in the LTC period . . . . . . | **21** |
22 Costs incurred for qualified LTC services provided for the insured during the LTC period (see instructions) . . . . | **22** |
23 Enter the **larger** of line 21 or line 22 . . . . | **23** |
24 Reimbursements for qualified LTC services provided for the insured during the LTC period . . . . | **24** |
Caution: *If you received any reimbursements from LTC contracts issued after August 1, 1996, see instructions.*

25 Per diem limitation. Subtract line 24 from line 23 . . . . | **25** |
26 **Taxable payments.** Subtract line 25 from line 20. If zero or less, enter -0-. Also include this amount in the total on Form 1040, line 21. On the dotted line next to line 21, enter "LTC" and the amount . . . . | **26** |

Form **8853** (2012)

Now, let's move on to a few limitations- those who can't participate and the things you *can't* do.

To participate in this type of plan you must be enrolled in both Part A and Part B of original Medicare. Even having met this requirement, there are certain individuals who cannot participate in MSA plans. Medicare eligible individuals who are covered by employer or union group plans that would pay the MSA deductible cannot enroll in an MSA. Medicare eligible individuals who are covered by Department of Defense Tri-Care cannot enroll in an MSA. Medicare eligible individuals who are covered by Federal Employee Health Benefits cannot enroll in an MSA. Medicare eligible individuals who are covered by Medicaid cannot enroll in an MSA. Medicare eligible individuals who have End Stage Renal disease or are in hospice care cannot enroll in an MSA. Medicare eligible individuals who live outside the United States more than 183 days a year cannot enroll in an MSA. So unlike various other types of Medicare coverage, *the MSA account requires the member's financial participation through the use of a deductible that cannot be covered by any other source except personal funds. This is a very good thing for those who choose to use the MSA because it ensures that the MSA member, who is part of an insured risk pool, is conscious of their expenditure and is compelled to make good decisions about who, when, how, why and where their healthcare dollars are spent.*

Is there anything that you should not do once enrolled in this plan? Yes! Once again: you must never spend the money put into your Medicare Savings Account on non-qualified expenses; Luckily, it is easy to distinguish qualified from non-qualified expenses: if an expense is not included in Publication 502, Medical and Dental Expense, from the IRS, this means that it is non-qualified.

If you do spend the money on non-qualified expenses, the penalty is significant. The tax penalty is 50% tax on the money spent on non qualified expenses. As bad as that may seem, the fact is you are giving back money that was given to you in the first place. With that said, you never want to expose yourself to liability or scrutiny by the IRS. Just follow the rules and you will never have to pay a dime of tax on the MSA deposits or expenses.

So as to review, let me outline the steps required to be part of a Medicare Savings Account Medicare Advantage plan from the tax filing perspective:

You must track all of your deposits and spending in your Medicare Savings Account. This is usually done in the same manner as a regular check book.

Annually you must file an IRS form 8853 for each account holder (husband and wife) with your regular 1040. Then you must file a combined form 8853 even if you are not required to file a 1040 due to your income.

That's it! Those are the rules that you need to follow in order to take advantage of the Medicare Savings Account Medicare Advantage plan. It couldn't be any easier!

(But I would caution you to consult with a CPA or tax professional if you are unsure of how to file because you do not want to cause an issue by filing your forms improperly!)

In this book, I am discussing the features of a generic MSA plan as designed by the law. As there can be many variations of the MSA by state, you should consult your state plan directly if one exists. In fact, most states do not have MSA MA plans available.

The MSA has two parts that make up the complete plan. The first part is a High Deductible Health Plan that provides coverage after you meet a calendar year deductible. The plan that I favor in down state New York has a $4250 deductible in the calendar year. This is the fully insured component of the plan providing the member stop-loss that cannot be exceeded within the calendar year. For the Medicare beneficiary this is the maximum out-of-pocket expenditure within the calendar year.

The second part of the MSA is the Medical Saving Account which is used to deposit cash funds provided by the contracted provider (generally an insurance carrier) for the beneficiary's use within the calendar year. The funds deposited in the Medical Savings Account can be used to pay for healthcare expenditures from January 1st to December 31st of the current calendar year.

This is a special fiduciary account that is set up by the insurance carrier who provides the High Deductible Health Plan. The MSA savings account is funded with $2500 each year and those funds can be used by the Medicare beneficiary for qualified medical expenses as defined by the Internal Revenue Service. (I suggest you order a copy of the list of qualified medical expenses for you use from the IRS.) When you spend the MSA funds on expenses that are considered Part A or Part B Medicare covered services, the High Deductible Health Plan deductible is reduced by the amount spent. The best way to understand the effect of spending money from your Medicare Savings Account on Part A & B expenses is that as you spend money from the MSA account the deductible goes down by the same amount. The CMS website has a very brief basic steps chart that I thought would be useful to reference on how a MSA actually works.

You can also request a copy of the entire CMS manual that explains how MSA Medicare Advantage plans work by sending an e mail to gfox@primordiainteractive.com.

As I wrote this book for the Medicare beneficiary who is unfamiliar with the MSA MA plan, I would say you should be cautious and always read your plan offering in your state carefully.

As explained in previous chapters, the Medicare Savings Account is a private insurance carrier's plan that provides all the same benefits as original Medicare but under contract with the Centers for Medicare and Medicaid. The MSA plan is a type of Medicare Advantage plan but provides coverage in a very different way than all other types of MA plans; *it is based on the model of Consumer Directed Healthcare as opposed to Coordinated Care.* Regardless, you will still have all the rights and protections that are provided by original Medicare.

Conclusions

THE SOLUTION IS Consumer Directed Healthcare: Why Medicare Savings Account is the Fix for Medicare Beneficiaries Needs!

Consumer-directed healthcare (CDHC) is center stage in health policy debates. Many politicians and corporate leaders hope that high deductible health insurance policies will cut costs by coaxing people to think twice before visiting the emergency department (ED), drug store, or MRI suite. The basic idea is that Americans are too well insured; if they spend their own money – so the logic goes – they will spend it more wisely (www.ncbi.nlm.nih.gov/pmc/articles)

This quote is over seven years old, and it was as true then and it is true now. What the entire article fails to address, however, is the economics of purchasing insurance and how that affects the delivery of healthcare. As I have stated many times previously, the decisions that are made concerning healthcare often revolve around cost. The primary reason for the proliferation of Managed Care Medicare Advantage plans is the perceived savings and the low premium costs. Those monetary savings come at a significant cost, in consumer-autonomy; consumers of these plans accept the promise of lower premiums at the expense of being controlled by a healthcare carrier administrator, a network restriction, or some other limiting factor. We also know now that the Managed Care model of health care will, in fact, not deliver the promised savings that were envisioned by the creators and administrators of the Coordinated Care Plans.

Consumer Directed Healthcare for the Medicare beneficiary is the only real solution ever offered under the current laws that can deliver on its stated goal of controlling costs. Moreover, it can only be obtained in the form of a Medicare Savings Account or MSA Medicare Advantage plan. What does having a MSA really mean for the Medicare eligible consumer of healthcare?

Freedom! Choice! Control!

And that is essentially what everyone wants in their healthcare coverage. Control over the who, when, where and what of how healthcare dollars are to be utilized. For the Medicare beneficiary there are three entities struggling for control of the healthcare dollars.

For the insurance carrier, it's about lowered costs through the use of managed networks that can be negotiated with the IPAs for lower costs by providing higher volumes of patients. For the IPAs, it's about banding together into groups of physicians to have negotiating power with the insurance carriers for higher payouts on the services they provide to the patients.

What results is a struggle between payers and providers for the one thing that I pointed out in the previous chapters; *it's all about the money and who will get it and who will save it.*

I just want to point out before I go any further: the struggle over the money is not inherently a bad thing. After all, the competition for your consumer dollars is what drives our economy.

As I stated before, it is to your benefit that your doctor and local hospital are wildly financially successful so that they have the capital to continue to innovate and improve the services that they provide.

But in this struggle between payers and providers, the most important element for healthy competition has been lost. That element is the consumer, the recipient of the healthcare services and the only meaningful reason to discuss healthcare to begin with. The consumer of healthcare must be at the center of this discussion. If consumer of healthcare is simply a secondary issue to the supply and demand equation between the insurance industry and the healthcare industry, then the system becomes broken.

When you choose to use a Consumer Directed Healthcare Plan you are putting yourself in the forefront of the healthcare delivery discussion because *you* are the payer and the manager of your own healthcare. This may seem to be an overwhelming task to someone who has had managed care for a long time, but you have always been in charge of your healthcare, just in an informal way. You chose your primary doctor. You got referred to specialist by asking your primary doctor "who should I see for this issue" and he gave you a name off a list that he uses. These are all the hallmarks of the types of skills required to succeed in using Consumer Directed Health Care to your advantage, you just didn't realize it at the time.

When you are in the Medicare System and you choose to use a Medicare Savings Account Medicare Advantage Plan, you are simply taking direct control of your healthcare instead of using a proxy that you call a network or insurance carrier. In choosing to have an MSA plan, you and thousands of others just like you are taking back their power in shaping the marketplace to become more responsive and more efficient to your needs instead of the needs of the insurance carrier or the IPAs. Those entities must now compete for *your* dollars, which *you* control because you decide the who, when, where, how and why in the healthcare decision-making process as it relates to you and your family. But most importantly, when you choose a Medicare Savings Account Medicare Advantage plan, you are changing the entire dynamic of your healthcare delivery because you will now be in control of cost, services, and access.

Finally, I want to point out that with all of this information you now have, you can be the most important thing when it comes to your health; and that is your own healthcare advocate.

Advocate for yourself when it comes to your healthcare and the first place to start is by using a Medicare Advantage Medical Savings Account.

Bibliography

"10 Basic Steps to Use a Medicare MSA Plan." *Basic Steps to Use a Medicare MSA Plan*. Medicare.gov, n.d. Web. 15 May 2013.

"The 100 Year-Old Debate: How Far Has Health Care Come?" *npr*. National Public Radio, 27 July 2009. Web. 28 Apr. 2013.

Baynes, Terry. "PRACTITIONER INSIGHTS." *WestlawNext Current Awareness*. ThompsonReuters News & Insight., 9 Apr. 2013. Web. 26 May 2013.

"Bill Text113th Congress (2013-2014)." *The Library of Congress*. N.p., n.d. Web. 10 May 2013

Bird, Julie. "Sebelius Acknowledges Tension between Care Coordination, Antitrust Laws."

FierceHealthcare. N.p., 10 Apr. 2013. Web. 26 May 2013.

"Calculators: Life Expectancy." *Social Security*. U.S. Social Security Administration, 03 June 2013. Web. 11 June 2013.

Commission to Study Social Insurance and Unemployment. Washington, DC: United States Congress, 1916. *Google Books*. United States Congress, House, Committee on Labor. Web. 11 May 2013.

"Costs & Financial Considerations in a Medicare MSA Plan." *Costs in MSA Plans*. Medicare.gov, n.d. Web. 11 July 2013.

Crandall-Hollick, Margot L. "The American Opportunity Tax Credit: Overview, Analysis, and Policy Options." *Federation of Scientists*. Congressional Research Service, 11 June 2012. Web. 11 July 2013.

"A Detailed Timeline of the Healthcare Debate Portrayed in "The System"" *PBS Online NewsHour*. PBS, n.d. Web. 11 July 2013.

"Expanded & Improved Medicare For All Act, H.R. 676." *Healthcare-NOW!* N.p., n.d. Web. 10 May 2013.

Gandel, Stephen. "What's the Purpose of Taxes?" *Business & Money*. Time Magazine, 16 Dec. 2010. Web. 29 May 2013.

"George W. Bush: Statement on Signing the Medicare Prescription Drug, Improvement, and Modernization Act of 2003." *George W. Bush: Statement on Signing the Medicare Prescription Drug, Improvement, and Modernization Act of 2003*. The American Presidency Project, n.d. Web. 26 May 2013.

"Healthcare in Germany." *Wikipedia*. Wikimedia Foundation, 21 June 2013. Web. 25 May 2013.

"The History of Medicare." *Social Security History*. U.S. Social Security Administration, 14 Dec. 2012. Web. 5 May 2013.

"Independent Practice Association." *Wikipedia*. Wikimedia Foundation, 18 Apr. 2013. Web. 12 May 2013.

"Information for Medicare Beneficiaries." *Information for Medicare Beneficiaries*. New York State Department of Financial Services, n.d. Web. 26 May 2013.

Internal Revenue Service. "Publication 969." *Interneral Revenue Service*. United States Department of the Treasury, Oct. 1997. Web. 29 May 2013.

Internal Revenue Service. "Publication 969." *Interneral Revenue Service*. United States Department of the Treasury, April 2000. Web. 29 May 2013.

Internal Revenue Service. "Publication 969." *Interneral Revenue Service*. United States Department of the Treasury, April 2001. Web. 29 May 2013.

Internal Revenue Service. "Publication 969." *Interneral Revenue Service*. United States Department of the Treasury, 2003. Web. 29 May 2013.

Internal Revenue Service. "Publication 969." *Interneral Revenue Service*. United States Department of the Treasury, 2012. Web. 29 May 2013.

Internal Revenue Service. "Publication 969." *Interneral Revenue Service*. United States Department of the Treasury, n.d. Web. 29 May 2013.

Johnson, Paul M., PhD. "Entitlement Program." *Glossary of Political Economy Terms*. Department of Political Science, Auburn University, n.d. Web. 15 May 2013.

Kusuma, Sharat, MD, Ryan M. Nunley, MD, James Genuario, MD, and Samir Mehta, MD. "Ahead of the Curve Issues Facing America: Consumer-directed Health Care." *AAOS Now*. American Academy of Orthopaedic Surgeons, Apr. 2008. Web. 11 July 2013.

Lynch, Wendy P. "Unless Consumers Demand Innovation, There's No End to the Rising Cost of Healthcare." *HCMS Group*. N.p., 27 May 2011. Web. 15 May 2013.

"Medicare Managed Care Manual Chapter 1 - General Provisions." *cms.gov*. Centers for Medicare and Medicaid Services, 01 Jan. 2011. Web. 28 May 2013.

"A More Secure Future." *Get the Facts Straight on Health Reform*. N.p., n.d. Web. 26 May 2013.

"National Health Insurance." *Wikipedia*. Wikimedia Foundation, 21 June 2013. Web. 26 May 2013.

"The Number of Workers per Medicare Beneficiary Is Falling." The Heritage Foundation, 22 Mar. 2012. Web. 11 July 2013.

Peikes, Deborah, PhD, Arnold Chen, MD, MSc, Jennifer Schore, MS, MSW, and Randall Brown, PhD. "Effects of Care Coordination on Hospitalization, Quality of Care, and Health Care Expenditures Among Medicare Beneficiaries: 15 Randomized Trials." *JAMA*. Journal of the American Medical Association, 11 Feb. 2009. Web. 26 May 2013.

"President Lyndon B. Johnson's, Remarks With President Truman at the Signing in Independence of the Medicare Bill, July 30, 1965." LBJ Presidential Library, 06 June 2007. Web. 29 May 2013.

Puckrein, Gary. "The Democratization of Health Care: The Force of Consumer Demand." *The Huffington Post*. TheHuffingtonPost.com, 04 June 2012. Web. 15 May 2013.

Schneider, Andrew. "Overview of Medicaid Provisions in the Balanced Budget Act of 1997, P.L. 105-33." *Cbpp.org*. Center on

Budget and Policy Priorities, 8 Sept. 1997. Web. 11 June 2013.

Weiner, Rachel. "Obama Health Care Speech: FULL VIDEO, TEXT." *The Huffington Post*. TheHuffingtonPost.com, 09 Sept. 2009. Web. 26 May 2013.

"William J. Clinton: Statement on Signing the Balanced Budget Act of 1997." *William J. Clinton: Statement on Signing the Balanced Budget Act of 1997*. The American Presidency Project, n.d. Web. 26 May 2013.

Woolhandler, Steffie, and David U. Himmelstein. "Abstract." *National Center for Biotechnology Information*. U.S. National Library of Medicine, 30 Mar. 2007. Web. 28 May 2013.

Suggested Resources

IRS Publication 969

IRS Publication 502

IRS Instruction 8853

IRS Form 8853

Fact Sheet on Medicare Medical Savings Account Plans

Your Guild to Medicare Medical Savings Account Plans

Active Saver MSA Plan Booklet

Has Medicare Been Privatized

Guidance for Medicare Advantage Medical Savings Account Plans

Medicare: History of Insolvency Projections

Press Release – CMS – July 10, 2006

Federal Register July 13, 2006

CMS Memo May 29, 2007

Where to get more information or enroll

THE MOST POWERFUL information is only as good as the action that is taken because of that information. Because you have made it to this page in the book, you obviously have interest in joining the revolution in Medicare by considering enrollment into a Medicare Savings Account. Now that you are aware of the MSA option, the next step for you is to request your enrollment kit or speak with a highly skilled agent who can guild you through the decision making process during the enrollment.

There are several ways to take action. Call our toll free number at 866 439 0964 and speak live with one of our agents.

Visit our webpage or Email your questions to admin@primordiainteractive.com

When you take charge of your life and more specifically, your healthcare; you are choosing to move forward with positive steps that will improve your life and your health.

But at the very least, exploring the possibilities offered by the Medicare Savings Account Medicare Advantage plan, you are taking the first steps toward taking control of your healthcare and your life.

Only good things can come from getting more information. You will either start a Medicare Savings Account Medicare Advantage plan or you will not, both ways you will be informed and acting as your own best advocate.

Event Registration Form

WE HOLD INFORMATIONAL events in various locations on a regular basis. The following form is included to allow you to register and attend a live event to get more information or meet directly with one of our representatives to discuss your specific situation. Simply complete the form on the following page and return it to us via email or fax. We will contact you to reserve your seat for one of our local events in your area when they occur.

Email : admin@primordiainteractive.com

Or

Fax to: (866) 901-7280

Name(s): _____

Address: _____

City:_____

State: _____ Zip:_____

Phone: _____ Email: _____

Medicare Effective Date:_____

Anything Else You'd Like Us to Know About You?
_____
_____
_____
_____

About the Author

GEORGE FOX WAS born and raised on Long Island, New York to a working class family. In his younger years his interests lied in following a career in agricultural science. Through his college education his interest expanded to business and eventually into the insurance field. It was in the insurance industry that he developed his true understanding for the need for individuals to have a clear view of the risk they face every day in all aspects of their financial life.

It was with this understanding that he began to work as a field underwriter for a major Insurance carrier which had a strong presence in the Medicare supplemental insurance market. After starting his career with one of the largest insurance providers of Medicare Supplement plans in the country, George rapidly moved to becoming an independent broker and has since been working continuously in the Medicare field as a broker and consultant.

When George entered into the senior insurance market, there were only supplemental insurance plans that wrapped around Medicare's primary coverage. Just a few years after entering the insurance industry the Balanced Budget Act of 1997 introduced the Medicare + Choice program. The senior market place would never be the same.

It was after Healthcare reform was finally enacted that George was able to realize his quest of providing beneficiaries with the most comprehensive coverage possible while providing complete control of the who, how, when and where beneficiaries would receive their care. It was the enactment of the Medicare Savings Account legislation and the subsequent development of an actual plan that enabled George to offer this coverage and which prompted him to pen this book.

Now that this legislative concept of the Medicare Savings Account has been brought from a law on the books to being an actual plan that you can participate in, this book will help you understand the time it took to get here and what you can expect in the future as you navigate the Medicare healthcare world.

As of the writing of this book George is an insurance industry veteran with over twenty three years of experience working with Medicare Beneficiaries. He holds all licenses in his field which include an LA, BR type.

George lives in Huntington, New York with his beautiful wife and three children. He can be reached by phone any time in his offices at (866) 439-0964 or gfox@primordiainteractive.com

www.ingramcontent.com/pod-product-compliance
Lightning Source LLC
Chambersburg PA
CBHW030009190526
45157CB00014B/1716